CAPTURE THE CULTURE

THE PROVEN PLAN TO RISE ABOVE THE CHALLENGES, BUILD A POWERHOUSE TEAM, AND TAKE YOUR BUSINESS TO THE NEXT LEVEL

CAPTURE THE CULTURE

THE PROVEN PLAN TO RISE ABOVE THE CHALLENGES, BUILD A POWERHOUSE TEAM, AND TAKE YOUR BUSINESS TO THE NEXT LEVEL

ERIN KRUEGER

ethos
collective

Printed in the United States of America

Published by Igniting Souls
PO Box 43, Powell, OH 43065
IgnitingSouls.com

LCCN: 2025901788
Paperback ISBN: 978-1-63680-456-9
Hardback ISBN: 978-1-63680-458-3
eBook ISBN: 978-1-63680-457-6

Available in paperback, hardcover, e-book, and audiobook.

Any Internet addresses (websites, blogs, etc.) and telephone numbers printed in this book are offered as a resource. They are not intended in any way to be or imply an endorsement by Igniting Souls, nor does Igniting Souls vouch for the content of these sites and numbers for the life of this book.

Some names and identifying details may have been changed to protect the privacy of individuals.

The superscript symbol IP listed throughout this book is known as the unique certification mark created and owned by Instant IP™. Its use signifies that the corresponding expression (words, phrases, chart, graph, etc.) has been protected by Instant IP™ via smart contract. Instant IP™ is designed with the patented smart contract solution (US Patent: 11,928,748), which creates an immutable time-stamped first layer and fast layer identifying the moment in time an idea is filed on the blockchain. This solution can be used in defending intellectual property protection. Infringing upon the respective intellectual property, i.e., IP, is subject to and punishable in a court of law.

Dedication

To my parents—
Though you are no longer physically here,
your presence is felt every day
in the lessons you taught me
through your actions, not just your words.
Your quiet leadership, unwavering support,
and example of integrity
have been my compass.
This book is a testament
to the values you instilled in me
and the culture you created.
I carry you with me, always.

Contents

Part One: Build Intentionally

Part Two: Nurture Consistently

Part Three: Monitor Actively

The Culture Guide[IP]

Foreword

When I founded Compass in 2012, I set out to create more than just a real estate company. Drawing inspiration from my mother, Ruth, a longtime real estate agent. I envisioned a brokerage built for agents, with a platform that would empower them to better serve their clients, combined with a company that would focus on culture above everything else. Over the years, I've had the privilege of working with some of the best real estate professionals in the industry, and among them is Erin Krueger. As one of Compass' top-producing agents, Erin embodies so many of the values that we hold at Compass and her success should come as no surprise.

I first met Erin six years ago, and from that moment, I could tell she was a remarkable person. At Compass, we value agents who are not only passionate about real estate but also committed to fostering an environment where their teams can thrive and where culture matters. Erin's commitment to this is a larger part of Compass' success in Nashville, and she has served as an inspiration to many across the country. Erin built and leads one of the most productive teams in Nashville, consistently delivering record results while creating a culture of excellence and collaboration in her business. Her team's success is not just a product of hard work but a testament to her ability to cultivate an empowering environment. This is what *Capture the Culture* is all about—understanding that success is born from leaders who build a culture that elevates people, inspires innovation, and fuels growth.

Over the years, I've had the opportunity to witness Erin's journey at Compass. Her passion for real estate and her dedication to her team are evident in everything she does. Erin's rise to become one of Compass' top agents isn't just a result of her talent—it's the result of her commitment to building a cohesive team culture. Seeing Erin on stage, speaking at Compass conferences, and watching how people look up to and admire her should tell you everything you need to know. She knows that great results come from empowering those around you, and she's mastered the art of leading by example.

One of the things that stands out most about Erin is her ability to achieve this success with a smaller, tight-knit team. Erin has proven that size isn't the key to success—leadership and culture are. Her focus on fostering strong relationships, both with her team and her clients, has propelled her to national and state recognition amongst all real estate agents. She is ranked among the top agents not just because she sells homes but because she has created an environment where her team members can grow and excel. This focus on culture is exactly why Erin's insights in *Capture the Culture* are so relevant and so needed in today's world.

Capture the Culture is more than just a book about business leadership; it's a roadmap for anyone looking to build something meaningful. In today's fast-paced, competitive world, having a strong culture isn't just an advantage—it's a necessity. Erin understands this better than anyone. Through her experience, she has crafted a blueprint for leaders, entrepreneurs, and real estate professionals to build teams that are not only productive but also deeply engaged and motivated. Whether you're leading a small team or a large organization, the principles in this book are universal. Erin's journey provides a clear example of how a strong culture can drive results and create lasting success.

For anyone in business, the message in this book is clear: leadership and culture go hand in hand. As leaders, we have the power to shape the environments in which our teams operate. Erin has done just that, and the results speak for themselves. The insights she shares in this book will challenge you to think about how you lead, how you inspire, and how you can create a culture that drives success in your own business.

Capture the Culture is more than just a guide—it's a call to action. Erin challenges all of us to rise above the everyday challenges of business and commit to building something greater than ourselves. By focusing on the culture we create, we can not only achieve success but also make a lasting impact on those we lead.

—Robert Reffkin
Co-founder and CEO of Compass, Inc.

Note to the Reader

Dear Reader,

Thank you for picking up *Capture the Culture*. If this book is in your hands, I believe it's for a reason.

Life has a way of challenging us in ways we never expect. I know what it feels like to face heartbreak, setbacks, and uncertainty. But I also know this: *difficult days don't define us—what we do with them does.*

Through every challenge, I've learned that true success isn't about individual wins; it's about what we build, who we impact, and the culture we create along the way. The strongest businesses, the most resilient teams, and the most extraordinary leaders aren't just driven by numbers—they are guided by purpose, fueled by trust, and a culture that empowers, uplifts, and creates lasting impact.

Whether you're building a business, leading a team, or pursuing personal growth, I hope this book equips you with the tools and inspiration to build with intention, lead with authenticity, and create something truly meaningful—something you and those around you can be proud of.

You are capable of incredible things. And no matter where you are today, you have the power to change course and shape your future.

I'm honored to be part of your journey.

With gratitude,
Erin Krueger

CHAPTER ONE

Defining Moments

The knock came during a meeting for my sorority. I was in charge of the pledges, and we were gearing up for a week of fun. So, you can imagine our surprise to find someone from campus security waiting on the other side of the door. "Hello, ladies. I'm looking for Erin Krueger."

"That's me," I said

"Your sister's basketball coach has been trying to get in touch with you. She needs you to call right away."

My energy drained, and I felt the blood rush from my face. Something terrible had to have happened. Why would my sister's college basketball coach be trying to reach me instead of my mom, dad, or sister? In an age when there was nothing smart about a cell phone, I'd left mine on my desk at my place across campus.

I raced back to the house I rented and climbed the stairs to discover I had forty-seven missed calls. Everything pointed to the worst, but I still didn't realize the gravity of the moment. The majority of the missed numbers belonged to my mom's best friend, Sue, so that's where I started.

"Erin, there's been a terrible accident."

My heart dropped.

"I need your roommates to start driving you home. There was a terrible accident after your sister's basketball game. Get in a car and head this way. Charlene and I will meet you half-way. We are leaving now."

That's all she told me.

My roommates got in my car with me, and we headed east. We had a four-hour drive across the state of Pennsylvania, and I had no idea exactly what news awaited me.

About an hour and a half into the trip, Sue called to see where we were. I had so many questions. My emotions got the best of me, and I just kept screaming. "Sue, I have to know. How are they? Are they alive? I have to know."

"Your mom and dad were driving home from the game. Your dad is gone, Erin."

I just started wailing. Devastation consumed me.

Finally, I asked, "What about my mom, Sue? Is she okay? What about Amy?"

"Amy was not in the car; she traveled with the team. Your mom is alive. But, Erin, it's not good. They had to rush her into surgery. We need to get you home as soon as possible."

My friends laid reassuring hands on my shoulders, and we drove as fast as we could toward Philadelphia.

Survival

Mom called me her "mini-me"—blonde hair, similar temperament. She got a kick out of it when we went shopping and people thought we were sisters. Much of who I am comes from my gorgeous, confident, and very direct mother.

When I walked into the ICU that day, I couldn't recognize my beautiful mother. The deer that had come through the windshield while on the Pennsylvania turnpike had killed my dad instantly and broken every bone in my mom's face. And though I didn't know it yet, the accident caused a spinal cord injury and left her a quadriplegic.

Over the next week, I planned my dad's funeral and advocated for Mom's health care. She had a long road ahead of her. There would be rehab, surgeries, and more—more medical decisions than I had ever imagined, and I was responsible for them.

So, when I walked into the ICU a week or so later and saw a bag of blood hanging, which no one had mentioned to me, I knew I had to take charge. I called a meeting with the medical staff and directors at the hospital. My mom's best friend, Sue, a registered nurse, went with me as I confronted the medical team.

"I know I'm only twenty-one, but I am the quarterback of this team. I need you all to talk to me, and I need to be able to make decisions." At that moment I took back the ability to drive the train, and every moment of my life since has been a reflection of that moment.

I needed to make many crucial decisions over the next few months. In addition to my mom's health care, I had a farm to think about. My dad had been a cattle farmer all his life. He raised and showed Angus beef cattle and owned one of the very few Triple Crown winners. This wasn't a hobby farm; it was our livelihood.

I knew my mom would need a tremendous amount of care. There was no way she could take care of the farm after she recovered. I had to figure out a way for my mom to live out the rest of her life comfortably as a quadriplegic. We had no choice but to liquidate to get rid of the debt and give my mom the kind of medical care she needed.

A few months later, with my mom still in the hospital, I sat at a table with a bunch of fifty-year-old men—attorneys and auctioneers—telling me I needed to have the dispersion sale for the farm in the spring. If we sold the cattle in April, we'd get the best price. I can't put into words the amount of stress the thought of selling caused. My heart started beating so fast.

"I need a moment, gentlemen," I said as I turned and headed into my dad's office. I quietly closed the door behind me, sat in his chair, and crumbled. I know they were trying to do what was best, but I just couldn't. I was going back and forth from college, caring for my mom with my grandparents' help, and now this. They wanted to have the dispersion sale in the middle of the semester. It was just too much.

Tom and Sherri were the executors of my mom and dad's estate as well as their best friends, and they followed me into the office.

"I just can't do this," I told them. "I'm traveling back and forth for school, trying to make decisions for Mom, and fighting to just finish this year and graduate. I can't think about hundreds of people being here on the property while I'm working to get through school." I dropped to my knees. I could feel myself breaking.

Tom and Sherri were actually more than just my parents' best friends. They were and are like second parents to me. At that moment, Sherri said to me, "You do what you need to do. We are behind you 100 percent."

I wiped my tears, stood up, and walked back into that kitchen to face those auctioneers, attorneys, and businessmen. Yes, they knew the market, but I knew my family and myself.

"The dispersion sale will happen in June after I graduate college," I said to them. "If that means the cattle don't look as good and we get less, then that's what's going to happen. I have to do what's best for our family, and right now, it's too soon and too fast. I just can't do it all. I would rather do this the right way than the rushed way, that is what my dad would have wanted."

Take Your Power Back

For the second time in my twenty-one-year-old life, I took back my power. It would have been easy in both instances to sit back and allow those who knew more about the situation to control the circumstances. However, that wouldn't have been what was best for me or my family.

I spent the rest of the year being a caregiver. I woke up very early every day and fed the cattle, returned to the house to get ready for the day, then drove to my internship in Public Relations. In the afternoon and early evening, I came home to care for my mom during the periods when home health aides or grandparents weren't able to step in and help. It was a lot. I made it through, but even so, it was pretty overwhelming.

The year shaped my perspective. When I go through trying times now, I can ask myself, "Is it as bad as that? Could it get worse?" It can always get worse. Three key attributes I call my "Survival Philosophy" help me get through difficult times. First, remain present. Just be where you are. Second, stay focused on what's best for you and those closest to you rather than what the so-called experts think. And third, make a decision and move forward. This philosophy has been my guiding principle.

We ended up dispersing the farm, and a few short months later, my mom passed. Almost a year to the day after the accident, we laid my mom next to my dad.

My mom and I had many great conversations when she was going through rehab. She often said, "Erin, I don't worry about you and where you're going." Her confidence in me was inspiring.

I'm sure she remembered the time I promised her she wouldn't always have to work so hard. Being a nurse and a farmer's wife meant she put in more hours than the average mother. I was very young when I told her, "One of these days, Mom, I'm going to be successful, and I'm going to hire a housekeeper for you and get you someone to take care of the yard." I wanted to be that person for my parents, and though I don't dwell on it, I still think about the fact I never had a chance.

One of the many conversations I had with my mom included how Nashville intrigued me. The city always seemed so interesting and appealing.

Fast forward to a trip to the country music capital not long after my mom's death. That's all it took. Nashville hooked me. I worked in marketing right outside of Philadelphia at the time, and when I got back to the office, I told my boss, "You have me for six more months. Then I'm moving to Nashville."

I didn't know a soul there, but I saw that as a positive. No one knew my story. I didn't have to be the young girl who lost her parents. Though that part of my life formed me and helped me grow, Nashville allowed me to start fresh.

Create a Positive Culture Regardless of the Ebbs and Flows

Farm life teaches many lessons, and tenacity might be one of the biggest. You can't quit on a farm. When you're sick, the animals still need to be fed. Vacations are often cattle shows. You don't clock out at five. You're done when the work is done. You keep going regardless of what the day looks like— good or bad, you push through.

The second powerful culture lesson I learned young is adaptability. Life is all about ebbs and flows. What you do with the low points and the high points, how you handle the climbs along the way, and which direction you pivot defines you and the culture you curate. My parents instilled in me tremendous ethics and attitude. I've carried many of their values into my adult life as well as my business.

Dad and Mom created a culture of communication, appreciation, and support without even knowing it. It's just who they were. However, their lessons have inspired me to build my business on culture rather than more traditional business strategies. I've discovered we can achieve extraordinary results when instead of working to become the best in the industry, each person on my team focuses on being the best they can be.

Whenever I bring someone new onto my team, I make them a promise. I will work with them, encourage them, and put them in positions for opportunities, but they have to do the work. We make a commitment to be better tomorrow than we are today.

And right here at the beginning of this book, I want to challenge you to embrace that goal to continually improve. Difficult days do not define you[IP]; what you do with them does.

I've been on quite a journey since that day the security guard knocked on the door of our sorority suite. I have a hard time finding adequate words to describe the transformational and deeply impactful path life has forged for me. But every event, regardless of the level of difficulty, has helped me grow. And now I want to share the lessons I've learned that can help you seize your future and Capture the Culture[IP].

PART ONE
Build Intentionally

CHAPTER TWO

Start with a Culture of Integrity and Knowledge

True to my word, six months after I gave my boss notice, I packed the car and headed south. At the same time, my sister was preparing to move to Georgia to attend Emory University for her Master's degree. Here we were, two twenty-year-olds convoying into unknown territory to live four hours apart and start fresh.

Alone in a new city, I found a townhouse, and within thirty days I had a job in advertising and marketing. I felt like I was living the dream, creating marketing campaigns for footwear and jewelry. This new city was good for me. It allowed me to start new and chart my own path. I had time to figure out who I was.

One day, a headhunter called and invited me to interview for a marketing-licensing position. I wasn't really interested, but when he called the second time, I figured what the heck.

Why not try? I never imagined that meeting would be so much bigger than a new position.

Another Pivot

My dad and mom were great mentors. They taught me how to work hard, give everything one hundred ten percent, make a list, cross everything off, don't do anything halfway.

I loved my childhood, but Dad always told me, "Erin, don't ever try to be a full-time farmer. Find another great career, then you can have a farm as a hobby." Full-time farm life means getting up early every day and dedicating all your days to the animals and the land. He wasn't saying this as though he hated what he did. He actually loved it, but some years were good, while others were a struggle. I carried their lessons with me through the rest of my life, and they served me well as I moved into this new world.

The headhunter I met with ended up being a retired Wall Street guru. Ed had lived all over the world and worked with many companies to grow them into public offerings. He landed in Nashville after retirement because he wanted to be near his grandchildren, and he and I just hit it off.

I ended up with that job as a marketing-licensing manager. This company filled its roster with young, bright, up-and-coming professionals. Most of the team had their Masters, and every person was expected to work day and night. They paid very well, so the hours seemed worth it. However, this was the first time in my work life I experienced burnout.

About eight months in, as I walked up the stairs on the first day back after vacation, I could feel the tension grow in my back, shoulders, and neck. I had already begun to realize the culture of the company wasn't for me.

On that day, the owner met me in the hall just inside the office door. He had a reputation for taking a perfectly calm office and creating chaos. He walked in, shook everything up, and left us feeling like we had to catch all the falling objects when he walked out.

Our company had been working on a new product; however, one of our competitors introduced something very similar and made it first to market. My boss' advertising plan was to copy the competitors' marketing strategy and use it to get our product out quickly. But this didn't sit well with me.

"We can come up with something better. It won't take long," I told him.

"Erin, you ARE just going to run with the plan." He would not take no for an answer. He even promised to give me my holiday bonus early when I was done.

Here I was once again, in my early twenties, going toe-to-toe with a fifty-year-old man. And this one was significantly more formidable than the doctors and the auctioneers.

I made my decision. "You'll have my resignation on your desk by the end of the day."

As I walked away, he yelled, "What are you going to do?"

I turned around and said, "I'm going into real estate."

At that point, that statement seemed to have come out of nowhere. But I had always loved real estate. I watched my grandparents and dad buy rental properties throughout my childhood. I didn't imagine being a realtor would ever be a full-time career for me. I pictured it as a side hustle or as a knowledge-as-power kind of thing, but it would at least be something to get me through until I found my next job.

As I spoke those final words, I felt hands on my shoulders. I knew that was my parents' pride resting on me. "That's our girl. She's making us proud standing up for what's right." You see, at the end of the day, all you have is your name, and that is important for me.

Never Sacrifice Integrity

Integrity remains a core value of my business. It's who I am—who I have always been.

When I graduated from high school, Tom and Sherri gifted me a week at their beach house with a few friends. On the last evening, I went over to see another group of friends who were nearby.

On my way back to the house, I noticed the road was jammed with cars. Soon, I could hear music blaring.

No way, I thought, *this can't be at my house.*

But it was. The driveway was full of cars, and there were people everywhere. I was in shock. All I remember is hitting the wall to turn the music off and yelling, "Everyone out of this house, now!" More than fifty people walked by me, leaving my friends standing there. "You, too." I told them.

"What do you mean? It's ten o'clock at night, Erin. What are we supposed to do?"

"Get your bags and get out."

I sat there feeling very alone and betrayed. Finally, I called my mom.

"I just kicked out my friends, Mom. The house is a mess," I told her after I explained what happened.

"You became an adult tonight, Erin. Your dad and I will be there in two hours."

Sure enough, they came and helped me put everything back together and clean up.

Even at eighteen, I knew what my friends had done wasn't right. Tom and Sherri treated me like their own. They had trusted me with their home. I lost a few friends that night, but I had to do the right thing.

Today, this sense of right and wrong stays with me, even when it doesn't always serve me well. For instance, when I represent the seller in a listing, and a buyer approaches me to be their agent for the same home, I will write the contract, but I make it clear to the buyer that they are unrepresented and that I represent the seller. My conscience just won't let me work for both sides.

If the buyer chooses to go through the deal unrepresented, I simply make sure they understand I'm obligated to act in the seller's best interest. I can't give them advice because I know the seller's end game. There's nothing illegal or even inherently unethical about representing both sides; however, for me it's a choice I made a long time ago on how I conduct business.

Everyone faces situations that challenge their principles every day. How you decide to handle those circumstances defines who you are and the company you are building. I believe creating a standard of the highest integrity allows me to be the best I can be.

People remember a culture of honesty that goes above and beyond the present-day norms. They appreciate you when you say, "I don't know," instead of trying to make something up. And they respect those tough conversations even when they're uncomfortable. It's not easy to tell a seller their house isn't worth as much as they think it is, but in the end, they appreciate the truth. Whether I'm dealing with my team or clients, I want to be known for a culture above reproach.

Find a Mentor or Two

I can't say it was easy to give up that Christmas bonus and walk out on a six-figure job with no firm prospect in front of me. But I felt confident about my decision.

When I started in the industry, real estate teams weren't really a thing. There were just a bunch of big powerhouse agents, and most weren't that collaborative. They didn't share successes, and they weren't about to meet you for coffee to give you tips or show you the ropes. But the person who sold me my house seemed different. Susan was a spitfire. And since I had just committed myself to real estate, I decided I wanted to work with her.

I called her almost immediately after I left the marketing job. "I'm going to get my real estate license," I told her. "Will you mentor me?"

After I got a yes from her, I called Ed. He had begun to coach me in the business world after our first cup of coffee. I don't think he was surprised to hear I had quit my job after I told him what transpired. I still appreciate the support he gave me more than twenty years ago.

Ed met with me once a month during the next several years to give me encouragement and advice on how to grow and excel in the business world, while Susan taught me the ropes for the first six months of my real estate career.

My first real estate deal was with one of the top realtors in Nashville. But I had no intention of letting him know I was that new. Honestly, I thought, *This real estate stuff is easy.* From that very first sale, I knew I was in the right place.

Two of my top lessons during that period were the importance of integrity and a support system. I have never regretted taking a stand on the side of right. And I don't know how I would have managed to grow as quickly as I did without Ed and Susan. That monthly cup of coffee and their guidance meant the world to me. A strong foundation of mentorship is key in building something great.

Embrace Knowledge as Power

I quickly found out my easy first deal may have lulled me into a bit of fantasy. In fact, my first few months in real estate made me feel pretty confident. The one lesson I hadn't learned yet was the difference between an hourly paycheck and a commission-based income.

When the housing market came crashing down in 2008, I went from six figures to eating ramen and trying to survive. The recession was tough. I had a mortgage and the stress of the other bills of adulthood. Regardless, I knew I had found my passion. I loved working in real estate. Learning its ups and downs was very good for me.

During this time, I continued to meet with Ed monthly. One conversation floored me. It felt like it came out of left field. But Ed's question completely changed the trajectory of my life.

"Erin, you're more than a realtor. You are an entrepreneur." Ed challenged me. "You have two options. Either go to law school or get your MBA. What are you going to do?"

"What do you mean, 'what are you going to do?' I work for myself. Why would I go to law school or get my MBA? It's not like either of those are going to get me an instant promotion."

"Oh, you're going to get a promotion." Ed reminded me of one of the tenets of my parents' lives—knowledge is power. And he continued, "Erin, you're an entrepreneur.

You're growing. This will help you grow faster." He wasn't going to let me leave that table until I made a decision.

I respected Ed so much, I knew I had to take action. Given my financial situation, pursuing an MBA felt like the practical choice—it was more time-efficient and financially feasible for me.

With the extra time the recession provided, I enrolled in University of Maryland's Global Campus satellite program. It was one of the best choices I ever made. To this day, my husband tells me part of the degree belongs to him for helping me get through statistics. But the opportunities afforded me because of this degree have been life-changing. This goes back to something I say every day on my team: Be Better Tomorrow[IP]. Be committed to being better tomorrow than you are today.

CHAPTER THREE

Stir in a Little Hustle

I didn't excel in academics. My SAT scores weren't Ivy League levels like my sister's, and I had to work really hard to get good grades. Nonetheless, every teacher knew my name. I sat up front in every class and always had my hand up. Even today, I may not be the smartest person in the room, but no one will outwork me. I guess I've always had a bit of hustle inside me. Keeping still isn't in my DNA. And this piece of me revealed itself in a big way during my MBA program. My final project required developing a business plan for something that had never been done before.

Healthy living wasn't at the forefront like it is now, but I saw so much obesity along with poor eating habits in schools that I decided my business plan would be based on healthy vending machines. The presidential administration at the time had begun to push health-conscious food choices in the schools, so it seemed like a timely idea. And when my professor saw the proposal, he encouraged me to make it more than just an assignment.

I'd already gone into my savings to pay for my MBA, and the recession didn't show signs of stopping anytime soon. But I still had a bit I thought would get us through the lean years, and I believed in myself.

What Happens When You Believe in Yourself

I ended up taking $30,000 from savings to create a company called Naturally Delicious, a brand based entirely around ambient vending machines. Each machine had a refrigerated section and a room-temperature shelf so school kids could get Fiji water or organic milk as well as pita chips, hummus, protein bars, and other healthy snacks all from one machine. The units used credit cards and sent me reports on what had sold so I knew when to refill them and what products they needed.

But bringing the idea of a vending machine into reality was just step one. Next, I had to find schools and gyms to put them in. I remember sitting outside a private school in Nashville, pumping myself up to walk in and convince the administration they needed healthy food options for their students.

I didn't have an appointment, and when I opened the door, I immediately saw the soft drink machines. The major soda company also sponsored the sign above their scoreboards in the gym. I knew this might be a tough sell.

But I didn't back down. I presented my idea to the main decision-maker. The older gentleman just smiled at me when I was done. "You remind me of my sister. She could have sold ice to Eskimos. You've got it. Your machines are in, and the soda machines are out." And just like that, I had my first contract.

Soon, the press picked up the news about the school introducing a healthy alternative, and more private schools contacted me about installing machines in their buildings. Before long, I had a contract for some of the area's public schools. Even a few local businesses and YMCAs added my company to their locations. My garage officially became my first warehouse.

As CEO and janitor, I came home every evening from my full-time job in real estate and downloaded the reports from each vending machine off my phone. My wonderful husband brought my dinner to the garage, and I ate while I organized products and figured out my route for the next day.

Then, every morning, I got out of bed at four, loaded my SUV, and headed out in jeans, sneakers, and a tank top under a branded zip hoodie. As Naturally Delicious Vending's sole employee, I spent those wee hours of the morning stocking vending machines. At nine, I unzipped that hoodie and swapped it for a blazer, kicked off the sneakers so I could put on my heels, and headed out to my first real estate appointment of the day.

The schedule was grueling, and I wasn't crazy about those cold winter mornings loading and unloading the SUV in the dark. But the side hustle helped me make ends meet while the housing market was down.

The business grew to the point I finally had to hire people to help me fill the machines, and after growing Naturally Delicious Vending to a large business with machines just about everywhere, I was approached about selling it.

By this time, the recession was slowing, so it was an amazing opportunity to put all that time into my real estate business. At the closing table, though, the buyer did try to renegotiate. I probably still looked young and inexperienced, but when the gentleman tried to change the terms of the deal, I just said, "Well, thank you for the non-refundable deposit." He quickly changed his mind and closed using our original agreement.

Within a few years of selling the vending machines, my hustle culture and the ability to focus on what I loved took me to number one agent in Tennessee and a rank of fourteen in the US for most homes sold by an individual agent. I sold over three hundred homes in a year, not long after I sold the business.

The Hustle Culture

Many think negatively when they hear the term hustle. They envision people burning themselves out, abandoning their families, and facing a million detrimental health effects. But you don't get big things and big opportunities unless you work hard. And I believe you can have a hustle culture without sacrificing your health or your family.

First, my hustle culture doesn't revolve around money—that's a by-product. What's important to me is service. As I mentioned, my parents emphasized giving one hundred ten percent. My dad didn't do anything halfway. Yet he still managed to make the hustle meaningful.

I remember hearing Dad's footsteps as he came in to wake me at five in the morning. He never said, "Let's go, time to get to work." Instead, he asked, "Do you want to help Dad today?" And together, we'd walk down to the cold barn. Dad would flip on the lights, and before we touched anything else, he always switched on the radio to the oldies station, reached out his hand, and he and I would do the jitterbug.

That's my kind of hustle culture. At 5:15 a.m., I felt revived because I laughed with my dad, and I was ready to help for the rest of the day. A good hustle makes it fun even when the job is tough. It means you're thankful for the smallest thing.

And like my work with my dad, a beneficial hustle is never demanding. Rather than tell the team what they have to do, I like to ask, "Can you help me with this?" I've never had anyone say no, because this kind of hustle means being appreciative, respectful, and showing your gratitude in big ways sometimes.

Maya Angelo said, "People will forget what you said. People will forget what you did. But people will never forget how you made them feel." When the hustle culture keeps this philosophy always in its sights, you can increase your productivity more than you imagined.

My dad always made me feel special and empowered. Even though he worked from before sunup to after sundown every single day, I never felt like the hustle was more important than our family. We worked together and had fun while we worked.

You can include hustle in your business culture; it simply needs to be monitored constantly. Plus, you have to be intentional. Always remember to Balance the Hustle[IP] with a bit of jitterbug.

The Energy Bus

Everyone has had at least one boss who acted like a jerk, and fortunately, if you have a growth mindset, you can learn as much from the jerks as you can from those who provide inspiration. After I walked out on the boss who asked me to copy another company's ads, I swore when I had my own business, I would make sure every person who worked with me never felt that dread of walking through the door at work.

It doesn't matter how much money you make if you're not surrounded by a good group of those who lift you up. Jim Rohn once said, "You're the average of the five people you spend the most time with." Who have you surrounded yourself with? Do they lift you up and empower you? Do they challenge you? Do they make you better or pull you down? Everyone needs to vent, but if a person tends to focus on their problems, do you really want to have that negativity influence you every day?

The Energy Bus by Jon Gordon is required reading for my team. It's full of little snippets on positive mindset. I love his analogy of life being a bus we drive wherever we go. He reminds us that complaining cannot take us forward. Only positive energy can send us in the right direction.

I aim for every person on my team to join me on the energy bus and support each other. This doesn't mean we won't have bad days or allow ourselves to have a minute or two to wallow in our misery; however, we never live there. You drive your own bus, and you can either join those who are fueling the Energy Bus and feed off their positivity, or you can become what Jon Gordon calls an Energy Vampire or what I refer to as Negative Nellies or Negative Nathans[IP].

These negative personalities can make a positive environment a place of dread if you don't monitor it. Instead of fueling the bus, they slow it down or put it in reverse. These people deplete the energy from culture and hamper productivity. Not only do you want to avoid being this person, but you should do whatever is necessary not to get on this person's bus.

When your culture includes this kind of positivity, people want to work with you. Your organization will grow organically because clients go out of their way to work with positivity. Your team won't mind putting in a little hustle because they'll love what they do, and they'll know you expect their hustle to be filled with positivity, energy, and balance—things people on the Energy Bus crave.

Mr. Gordon summed up this theme nicely. He said, "The best legacy you could leave is not some building that is named after you or a piece of jewelry but rather a world that has been impacted and touched by your presence, your joy, and your positive actions."[1] This is the kind of culture I seek to create, and I work hard to protect it every day.

---

[1]   Gordon, Jon. *The Energy Bus.* Wiley and Sons: New Jersey. 2007.

CHAPTER FOUR

You Can't Do It Alone

Three hundred home sales as a solo agent in one year is crazy. Ask anyone in the business and they'll agree. Reaching number one agent in the state and ranking nationally became another pivotal moment in my career—not because of the status but because I discovered I couldn't keep up that pace on my own. I realized if I wanted to keep hitting goals, I needed to pivot again—it was time to build a team.

Real estate teams weren't a big thing when I started. There may have been a handful in Nashville. So, I really didn't know what I was doing. I didn't know how to hire. I didn't know how to scale.

But I was growing, and I had a vision. I wanted to keep getting bigger and still do excellent work, so I knew I had to have a good group to help me reach my goals.

My first hire was a mistake. I realized it almost immediately, and that person didn't last a week. I had to come up with a better plan than "find a warm body" if I wanted to scale.

Put Processes in Place

After I gave myself a little pep talk, I started really thinking about the things I needed if I wanted to take myself from an individual agent to a real estate business. What kind of people did I need to help me reach my goals? What did I want the job descriptions to look like so I would have a blend of people with various talents? What do I want a team to do after I hire them?

Sharon was my first pivotal hire. A licensed realtor, she also had experience in transaction management. With her help, we created systems and processes and came up with an outline for many areas of the business. The checklists we created became the foundation for our team. Sharon pulled my ideas out of my head, added to them, and organized them.

When I mentor people as they start their own business, I tell them to take out a voice recorder and just start talking about all the different steps they take during each transaction or task. If they've grown to the point where they need a team but have all their processes locked in their brain, they just need to talk it out and get it on paper so they can communicate their process to those they bring on.

The main goal for my business and my team is to be better tomorrow than we are today. These checklists help achieve that. They give us goals to reach and help us see when we fall short.

Those checklists will need to be reviewed and refined on a regular basis so they grow and evolve with your business. As you add members to your team and the dynamics change, the systems may need to be adapted to fit the growth. I don't need twelve or fifteen people who do things like me. I need a dozen team members who can put their own spin on my processes.

However, I have to communicate my processes if I want my team to succeed. This way the products and deliverables are always the same. The way they get done may differ depending on the personality providing the service, but the high standards never waver. Clearly defined processes allow the team to function at the highest level.

Everyone Needs a Georgia

I remember the day that Sharon came to me and told me she was leaving. Her kids were school-aged and growing, and her husband had a growing business. She wanted to help his company grow. I had leaned on Sharon since we started together, but she told me not to worry, she had found the perfect replacement.

At the time, I would have described Georgia as a Tasmanian Devil. I expected an organized assistant, but she was all over the place. She didn't have transaction management experience, but she was a licensed realtor and had the best presence. She was positive, funny, and eager to learn more, so I took a chance. I needed a Georgia, and obviously, Sharon knew it. Georgia is so much calmer than I am. She knows how to help me take it down a couple of pegs. It didn't take long for Georgia to become my right hand.

She was a licensed agent with a solid foundation—thanks to a broker mentor—but she was still refining her skills at the time. As my right hand, her main job was transaction manager. I had no idea how to hire and didn't know how to pay. In fact, I'm pretty sure I underpaid her back then. With just the two of us in the office, she had no choice but to hear me on all my calls. Before long, she knew what I was thinking even before I thought it.

Georgia has become a vital person in my professional career as well as my personal life. She is my sounding board. We all need someone to speak the truth into our lives—someone who will tell us when we're wrong or out of line. And this person should also care enough to have hopes and dreams for us and the team that are even bigger than we envision for ourselves. Georgia is one of those people, and I know she feels the same with me.

Through the years, Georgia has transformed. When we met, she faced a tough period in her life, but she has since come out stronger. I'm not sure she knew who she was outside the circumstances of her life. But she had definite goals. She was looking for something new and wasn't going to allow that moment in time to define her.

Today, she's a powerhouse. She smashes every goal and has moved into the role of senior buyers' agent and mentor to the younger agents.

Plus, she's fun and a joy to work with. She always says, "If it's not fun, I don't want to do it."

We know not every day will be a great day. Working with the public is rough sometimes. But when you have a "Georgia" on your team, you have someone who inspires you to put your Positive Pants[IP] on.

Sharon started our vital team checklists, but Georgia put them on steroids. She helped me see that not everyone will do things the way I do them, but at the end of the day, it will be done at the level our clients deserve. She reminds me we set up the process for the integrity of the company. So, as long as they're following the process, I need to loosen my hold on things and let others be themselves and flourish.

I'm a perfectionist. Georgia helps keep me grounded when things go a little haywire. I'm fast-paced—remember, I'm from outside Philadelphia. Georgia, along with my southern husband, calms me—though she still says I talk too fast. She's definitely not my clone, and she may not be perfect, but she's perfect for me. She keeps me balanced. So, you'll often hear me say, "Everyone needs a Georgia."

Not Just Anyone, The Right One

One of the keys to building a team is understanding the need for variety. The way Georgia and I work together is just one point of proof. If you were building a basketball team, you wouldn't want a bunch of Kobe Bryants. He may have been the leader, but would he have risen to greatness without the assists? Without a pro in every position, could his team have won so many games? You need people who excel in their specific area and can support everyone else on the team.

We start by asking, "Who do we need to bring this together?" Our company uses the DISC profile as a starter. Right now, we have the one who Dominates, the Influencers, a few who remain Steady, and many who excel in Conscientiousness. I want people around me who complement me and complement others on the team. Creating this blend brings a richness we would miss if everyone were the same.

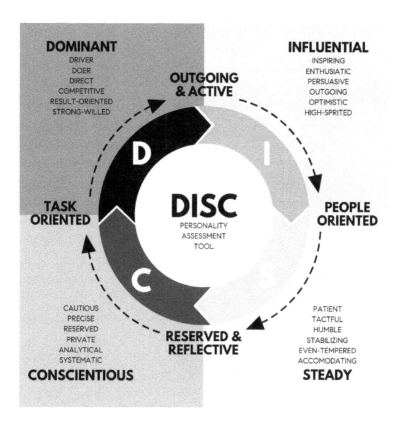

My team members have come from a number of places. And my early hires weren't nearly as intentional as they are now. You'll often hear the team members who've been with me the longest joke about meeting me for coffee at my "office" at Whole Foods.

Georgia came by way of an exercise class she took with Sharon, and Cat came through an unsolicited email.

Cat moved to Nashville from Chicago, and even before she hit the town, she sent me a message. She was relocating and wanted to interview with the city's top five agents. I didn't really need anyone at the time, but I truly appreciated her courage to cold call email, so I set it up.

We met for coffee and connected right away. And though I knew I'd have to turn her down, I told her to call me on Monday because I was heading out on our annual team trip. After the long weekend, I was positive I couldn't take leads away from my team. They had to be my first priority. But I invited her to keep in touch; now just wasn't the right time.

Cat signed on with a different agency after our meeting. But about two months later, she called. Things weren't working out at the other firm. She just wanted some advice.

We chatted for over half an hour before I told her the workload on my team had changed. I needed someone in administration. She hadn't worked in that area before and didn't have any networking connections in Nashville, but she learned fast. She met every goal she set and moved quickly into a buyer's agent position.

As the team grew and Georgia began to hit her stride and move into the sales area, I realized I needed someone to run the office—a Director of Operations. I had a full-fledged business, and I needed someone to oversee it. Cat had an idea.

"Erin, I know someone I think would be perfect. I have a friend I think you should talk to."

"Cat, we don't hire our friends. I know we're all friends here. But we've grown this relationship. We can't just bring in all the people we like." I could see how making friendship the basis for hiring could turn into a bad ingredient in the team.

"No, Erin, you really have to at least interview her."

I gave in. I met with Cat's friend, and very quickly I knew she would be valuable to our team.

Sarah started as my Executive Assistant. Even before her thirty-day review, I knew she was way overqualified for the job. So, when we sat down for that evaluation, I was honest with her. I think I even teared up as I started to explain how much I wanted her to grow with our team.

The promotion and raise proved to be exactly what she needed, affirming that we recognized her talents and valued her contributions. Sharing our vision for the company with her as an integral part empowered her to step up, embrace her potential, and make a significant impact. This was exactly what our team needed. As Director of Operations, Sarah helped take the Erin Krueger team to new heights. When I'm hyped up on big entrepreneurial dreams, she is calm, cool, and collected. She continues to contribute on such a high level for our team. By focusing on the right people, we hit our stride as a team.

Experience Versus Coachability & Trust

Often, companies will put an emphasis on experience and skills when they start building their team. And while qualifications will always be vital, at the end of the day if a person doesn't add tremendous character to the team, it's not going to be a good fit. Training is the easy part of developing a new hire. But I can't teach anyone a personal foundation of positivity, coachability, and a willingness to learn.

Laura provides a great example of this. She's known me longer than anyone else on the team. I met her when she was eleven, and I sold her parents their home at the very beginning of my real estate career.

I met her family when they moved from Jersey to Nashville. When I got the call, they told me they had a two-day deadline for finding a home. The pre-teen Laura was not nearly as excited as her younger sister to be uprooted from the East Coast to Tennessee. Even today, though I don't remember it, Laura talks about how mean she was to me because I was the one selling them their new house.

But from the beginning, I adored Laura. The dynamic between the two sisters reminded me of me and my sister Amy. And as I do with my clients, I kept in touch with their family. During Laura's college years, my husband and I were over for dinner and I asked her mom what Laura was doing for a college internship. I knew she wanted to be a lawyer.

"She's interning at a daycare," her mother said.

"What does a daycare have to do with being an attorney? I have an idea. Can you have her call me?"

Laura called, and I talked to her about being an assistant and a runner for our office as well as our compliance coordinator. This would give her the opportunity to review contracts and learn a bit about the legal side of real estate. I also offered to write a letter of recommendation to help her get a position in one of the congressman's offices. "This will put you in a good position to get into law school."

The next day, she quit her job and became a team assistant. Her greatest asset was her willingness to do anything and learn everything. I felt a moment of pride knowing I had watched her grow up and I had been able to see her potential.

As she got closer to going to law school, Laura moved to DC to take an internship with a law office. I was sad to see her go, but it only took two months for her to realize she didn't want to be an attorney. She wasn't sure what she wanted to do, but she had ruled out law.

When she called to tell me, I let her know we needed a transaction coordinator. This position is foundational to real estate. Since she wasn't certain she wanted to stay in this industry, I knew this would be the perfect place for her to start. It would give her a good foundation for whatever she wanted to go into later.

Laura flourished. She was extremely organized and thorough. After six months, she asked if it would be beneficial for her to get her license. I told her it would definitely be a positive move. She got her license but continued in transaction management. At the same time, she took a few leads, helped with open houses, and did whatever it took to grow her skill set.

That's the one thing I knew would take her far—her positive attitude and dedication to growth. These are key ingredients for any hire.

You can't make people do things. You have to inspire people[IP].

Laura has seen every aspect of my career. From the time I began as an independent solo realtor and then built my team, she has witnessed it all. She's seen the struggle—the highs and the lows.

Fast forward to today. She's taking on more and more deals and helps with many aspects of the business. When I need something done and done to the highest standard, I know I can ask Laura. When our marketing position was vacant, Laura was busy with buyers, but she stepped up and picked up the slack without me asking. She is an example of a true team player. She is a born teacher, like her mother, and is an excellent mentor and Customer Relations Management (CRM) wiz who helps teach the value of a well-organized CRM to our agents.

I believe everyone has opportunities to step up or step out all the time. Laura always steps up. Her spirit to serve makes me incredibly proud. When you look for a person to add to your team, ask yourself if they are coachable and you can trust them. I would much rather have a team member I can trust who is open to learning than an untrustworthy, high performer. A team member that has these qualities far outweighs any experience. The willingness to learn and a coachable mindset will allow the expertise to happen over time. By focusing on trust, you give yourself a strong foundation for any working relationship. Plus, with that kind of relationship, the people you hire become high performers in no time, just like Laura.

Our Hiring Evolution

Sarah was instrumental in changing the way we did our hiring. Instead of looking to friends and people we worked out with at the gym, we put hiring practices in place like a real business, I call this The Culture Fit Hiring[IP] process.

First, when someone sees one of our openings online, they'll find a detailed job description accompanied by instructions to send their DISC profile with their resume and references to Sarah. We don't tell them where to find the DISC profile, and we don't consider those who ask how to find it. We want to see if they have a basic level of problem-solving skills and an ability to follow instructions. You'd be amazed how often we get resumes without the DISC or references.

Then Sarah uses the DISC as a guiding tool to get the list down to seven or eight resumes and does a Zoom interview with each one. She narrows the list to three to four for me to meet. This meeting with me, whether it's on Zoom or in person, feels much like a typical job interview. I have a list of questions I use to screen for someone who fits our culture, and I'll include that list at the end of this chapter. However, in the middle of the interview, the candidates get a second test that has served me very well.

I explain the priority our team places on goals. At the end of every calendar year, we sit together and craft these milestones. Then, in June, we review them. Are we on track? Do we need to recalibrate? Have we already reached them and need to shoot for something higher? We look at the economic environment and the current state of our business. Have things changed? Do we need to pivot? This kind of heavy review means we need every new team member to understand the importance of goal setting.

I tell every candidate, "Goals are extremely important, and they are nothing unless you write them down. So, I want to know what your goals are. This doesn't have to be a thesis. I just want a couple of bullet points. I want to know, if we bring you on this team, what would have to happen to make you proud to sit across from me a year from now? What milestones would you need to reach? I want you to take a little time to think about it and email those to me tonight." Did you notice the time frame I mentioned? That is the test. I expect an email that evening.

Our team needs people who listen. I can teach you real estate, but I can't teach people to listen. I adapted this test from an impactful interview I had about a year after my parents' accident. Though I didn't take the position, their process stayed with me. The job was with a pharmaceutical company, and they had four rounds of interviews. The final one was in a restaurant, and at the time, I didn't even realize it was part of the test.

Back then, a big part of being a pharmaceutical representative was wining and dining doctors. They wanted to see if I reached for the salt and pepper as soon as the food arrived or if I took a bite to see if it really needed extra seasoning. Did I assume, or did I assess? We know what it means if you assume.

I respectfully declined the job because, at the time, I thought a high-pressure pharma job was too much too soon after my mom's death. Regardless, their unusual hiring process inspired me to come up with something that would help me identify the most qualified candidates.

Usually, at least one of the candidates I interview will either forget to send their goals or send them late. So even if the rest of the interview was amazing, those people are automatically out. I can teach you many things, but I can not teach you to listen. Listening is the number one thing in negotiations. If you don't listen, how can I trust you will listen to our clients?

After we've narrowed down the pool to two or three candidates with these few steps, I look for the one who is the most coachable and best culture fit. Who is willing to learn something new? Which candidates are willing to pivot? We're looking for team members who want to be better tomorrow than they are today. So, I consider the interviewees most likely to embrace our values and culture. Finally, I consider their attitude and mindset. The applicants who meet those qualifications then get to meet the team.

That's the final round of our process. Prior to putting this three-round interview in place, I had a hire that didn't work out. After about a year, we had to let her go, and one member of the team came to me and said, "I knew that person wasn't going to last. She didn't work like the rest of us. She just didn't fit in." I didn't want that to ever happen again. Our team needs to know we're in this together. I need complete buy-in, and when everyone is on the same page, the success rate is much higher.

To avoid having another team member that doesn't fit, the team gets the final say. I tell the applicants, "If you make it to the next round, you'll get to meet the team." And the two that make the final cut, hear me say, "I want you to interview this team as much as they interview you. Please ask any questions you want about what it's like to work for me. Because if we offer you the position, we want you to be an integral part of this team. Every person on the team will be pouring into you."

At the end of the interviews, each team member texts me and Sarah either yes or no and why. They will be taking precious time away from their own deals to nurture this new person, so we need a one hundred percent buy-in. By the time we hire, every person on the team has a vested interest in helping the new person grow and understand her opinion matters.

We don't discuss it around the table; there are no peanut gallery conversations. I want each person's gut instinct.

Much of the success of my company has come on the back of gut decisions. I have to make decisions fast. Good, bad, or ugly, I cut to the chase and then move forward. Even if I choose the wrong option, I move forward.

Your most important asset is your culture, and you have to protect it at all costs. Taking care of your team and making sure you have the right people in place is a crucial piece of the puzzle. Clients feel it when your people are happy. I want my team to thrive. Real estate deals with difficult life events. Many clients have faced fire, death, divorce, downsizing, and more. Great agents become master problem solvers. Test number one helps us weed out those who won't be able to fill this qualification.

Regardless of your industry—it might be a salon, a tech firm, or a Fortune 500 company—the culture you create with the people you bring on board will determine whether you keep moving forward or get stalled when a recession hits or some other company steals your idea. To Capture the Culture, we look for people with a positive mindset. We want to fill our team with members who individually set ultra-high goals—something else test number two reveals. And we want people who will work together for the common goal.

Culture Fit Interview[IP] Questions

These questions are designed to determine if the applicant is a good culture fit. You may need to modify them for your situation, especially if you have W2 employees rather than 1099 contractors. Before you begin, it's important to outline who you are and how you operate so the candidate can understand the culture and value your organization provides. Done right, the interview can help you find not only the technically qualified but also the right cultural fit for your company.

1. **Core Values**

   Question: What core values guide your work and decision-making? Can you give an example of a time you had to make a difficult decision based on those values?

   Purpose: This question reveals if the candidate's guiding principles align with the values your company holds dear.

2. **Understand and Embrace the Company's Mission**

   Question: What excites you about our company's mission, and how do you see yourself contributing to it?

   Purpose: Determine if the candidate is genuinely motivated by the company's purpose and whether they can see themselves as part of that vision.

3. **Collaboration and Teamwork**

   Question: Tell me about a time when you had to work closely with a team. How did you ensure collaboration and communication were effective?

   Purpose: Team dynamics are crucial to culture. This question helps you assess the candidate's priority regarding collaboration as well as his or her communication skills.

4. **Initiative and Ownership**

   Question: Can you describe a situation where you went above and beyond in your role? What motivated you to take initiative?

   Purpose: Culture fit often involves looking for employees who take ownership and don't shy away from responsibility. This helps identify if the candidate has a proactive mindset.

5. **Feedback and Continuous Improvement**

   Question: How do you handle constructive criticism? Can you share an example of feedback you received and how you acted on it?

   Purpose: A strong company culture thrives on growth and feedback. This question uncovers the candidate's openness to learning and self-improvement.

6. **Fit for the Company's Preferred Work Style** (e.g., independent vs. collaborative)

   Question: Would you describe yourself as someone who works best independently or in a team? Can you provide an example of a project where you worked this way?

Purpose: Different companies have different working styles. This helps you determine if the candidate can adapt to the way your company operates.

7. **Stress and Pressure**

   Question: How do you manage stress and tight deadlines? Can you share an example of a particularly challenging project and how you handled it?

   Purpose: Understanding how someone deals with pressure can indicate whether they will fit well in your work environment, especially if it's fast-paced or high-pressure.

8. **Commitment to Work-Life Balance and Company Well-Being**

   Question: What does work-life balance mean to you, and how do you ensure you maintain it?

   Purpose: This helps assess if the candidate's approach to balance aligns with the company's culture on well-being and flexibility.

9. **Alignment With the Company's Leadership and Communication Style**

   Question: Describe your ideal manager. What leadership style motivates you to do your best work?

   Purpose: Different leadership styles resonate with different people. This question helps determine whether the candidate will thrive under your company's management approach.

10. **Growth and Development**

    Question: Where do you see yourself in three years, and how do you think this role will help you get there?

Purpose: A culture of continuous growth and development is essential for thriving teams. This question reveals whether the candidate is committed to their own development and sees the role as part of that journey.

11. **Final Question**

Question: Based on what we've discussed today, how do you see yourself fitting into our company culture?

Purpose: This gives the candidate a chance to reflect and provide a final thought on why they believe they are the right fit.

Observational Assessment

Pay attention to the way candidates respond:

- Are they enthusiastic and thoughtful, indicating a genuine passion for their work?
- Do their examples show alignment with your company's core values and work environment?
- Are they respectful, communicative, and open-minded in how they speak about teamwork and leadership?

The Listening Test[IP]

Ask the candidates to "send your goals tonight" or send xyz before noon tomorrow. Their ability to carry this out will be revealing.

PART TWO
Nurture Consistently

CHAPTER FIVE

Mentoring and Growth

In my industry, maintenance is a must. Nothing deteriorates faster than an abandoned building—except perhaps an underappreciated team with a Lone Ranger culture.

When the team was small, maintaining the culture was easy. But the bigger we grew, the more difficult the task became. In fact, I've had stressful days when desperation tried to talk me into scrapping the whole thing and going back to a three-person office. I have a lot more overhead now than when I met people at my free office at Whole Foods. However, my real estate team is a powerhouse I could never be on my own.

Capturing the Culture turns into a business growth strategy. Fear of changing a tremendous culture can stunt your growth if you let it. When you have a tight culture like Georgia and I had in the beginning, you worry about what will happen as you add new personalities. Natural growth demands more staff, but how will you keep that close-knit relationship a high priority in your culture?

After you build a team of the best in the business, it's vital to nurture it. Maintaining a healthy team culture doesn't happen accidentally. But when the leaders purposefully Capture the Culture, it easily trickles down and permeates the company.

Become a Mentor

When I started, I had no idea how to run a team. And though I haven't had hits every time, I've learned from my mistakes. I love being hands-on and feel blessed to have been able to bring together such an amazing group of women.

I've already said I don't know what I would have done without my mentors, Ed and Susan, but I think one key to the success of our team is this idea of mentoring. Even back when I worked in advertising, I liked being able to empower people. As the Senior Advertising Executive, I was in charge of the interns. I told those young people, "Come help me do this project; you're going to be more than just the coffee gopher here." When I became a team lead, I wanted the junior agents to feel like they were with me rather than working for me. I wanted my team to have a "we" mentality.

In fact, when I am doing a deal with an agent who I can tell is new to the business, I like to be encouraging. When I hear the voice quiver or notice a lack of confidence, I take a minute to break the tension. "We're going to have a great transaction. I am excited to work with you." I want people to love what they do. I don't look at anyone as competition. We're all in this together. It's about collaboration.

A big part of mentoring includes training and coaching. We want each person to become the best version of themselves, so we give them all the tools they need. Companies that expect their staff members to learn on their own miss out on a huge part of growing the culture.

Raise Up Mentors

Today, our team has grown to the point I can't personally mentor each person one-on-one. I still have an open-door policy, do group coaching, and communicate with every member of my team, but new team members will not get the experience Georgia, Laura, and others have received by being glued next to me over the years. While this may seem detrimental, it actually builds the team as others step up to become mentors. Our team culture won't allow us to let another team member fail. We aren't individual agents out there in competition; we have team goals. Georgia, Loren, Laura, Mary, and the other senior agents take time out of their sales time to invest in our junior agents.

Years ago, we had an opportunity to advertise on Nashville buses. People were relocating from everywhere to our city, so I came up with the slogan, "Tourist Today, Local Tomorrow." The brokerage's marketing department did some art for me, but it didn't feel right. My marketing and operations directors, as well as our summer intern, Lindsey, were with me at the meeting, and we kept trying to explain what we were going for.

Finally, Lindsey raised her hand and said, "Erin, I've kind of been working on something. Can I show it to you?" When she let Sarah and I see her work, my mouth hit the floor. It was exactly what I wanted. In fact, that design is still on our buses in Nashville today.

It's this culture of mentorship and the message of "your voice matters" that gave her the courage to speak up. When

Lindsey came to us, she was super quiet. But being with my team of mentors empowered her to speak up in a room full of senior personnel. Creating a collaborative and open environment is key for growth.

Mentoring creates a space where people can share freely. Whether it's a good idea or a bad idea, they realize it needs to be shared. Someone else on the team might be able to build on it, and no one worries about not getting credit. There is no "I' in "we" culture.[IP]

You'll seldom hear the word "I" in our office. When a goal is met, "we" did it. I discourage anyone from saying, "Erin did this." That vernacular makes every client want to work only with me, and we have amazing people on the team who can accomplish as much, if not more, than I do. Because we all use the same systems and processes, every person has the same ingredients to be able to give the client a phenomenal experience.

Making the Investment

Investing in our team members is a major part of our culture, and education is an essential part of that investment. Each new member of our team receives training and learns scripting from senior agents. Some who look at the number of leads we get each year might assume when you sign on as a team agent, you just get a bucket of leads, but that couldn't be further from the truth. We want to set new agents up for success, so each new team member works side-by-side with a seasoned agent until she can effectively make an impromptu presentation in front of me and the other agents. Being prepared, being able to overcome objections, and delivering our value are key to becoming a valued and trusted advisor.

At one of our weekly meetings, I'll surprise the new team member with a short quiz and a bit of role-play. We want to make sure every person in our organization is prepared when they move to the next level and begin taking leads. I can tell you they don't like it. Some even dread it. It's difficult to be put on the spot in front of your peers and your boss. But it makes them so uncomfortable because they are growing and improving. These moments mold and shape them to the best they can be. I want them to be prepared for that day when I or the senior agents are not there.

Even an agent who's been in the industry for ten years often needs coaching and one-on-one training to ensure they can handle any kind of lead that comes their way. We want them to feel confident and have the tools they need to be an advisor to our clients. We believe knowledge allows us to provide more value to our buyers and sellers. And if we're valuable, we'll have clients for life.

Capturing the Culture means the education never stops. I learn every day. I am thirsty for knowledge. I want to be better—a better agent, better boss, and better professional— and if I stay committed to being better tomorrow, I will have better results. To keep the entire team at the top of our game, every Tuesday, one senior member leads a scripting session. They spend an hour coaching and mentoring. Then, immediately following, I join them for what we call "Erin Krueger Team University." We do a case study of sorts of a transaction I or one of our agents has been part of. We talk about industry changes everyone needs to be aware of, and we help prepare one another to be our best selves for our clients. I want them prepared, seasoned, and ready for anything that comes their way. I always say, "The harder I work, the luckier I get." It's important to remember—preparation meets opportunity.

A Culture of Encouragement

A "we" culture means each person gets excited for everyone else's success. Our team operates on leads. In fact, we are a lead-generating business. Calls come in from around the country daily—soft leads, referrals from past clients and agents from other markets, people who follow us on Instagram, and more. One stream of leads comes through on each team member's phone simultaneously. They're set so my phone vibrates just a few seconds before the rest of the team. Because part of our culture involves being available, each woman tries to be the first to answer.

That might sound highly competitive to the average company, but each member of The Erin Krueger Team competes with herself, not with her team members, because each of us is committed to being better tomorrow than we are today.

I love watching the group when we're all together in the conference room and I see one of those leads light up my phone. The agent who answers first leaves the room and enters one of our phone booths to talk with the prospective buyer or seller.

Our commitment to encouragement means that when our colleague walks back in and announces she has a consultation with a new buyer the next day, the entire team cheers. Her success is our success. And because we focus on encouragement rather than competition, should the call include an aspect that falls in another agent's wheelhouse, the first person to answer now has an instant mentor.

For instance, if the buyer is looking for land or has a specific niche, and another team member is more seasoned in that area, the two collaborate. One member becomes the mentor, and the other soaks up every bit of information they can so they improve in every area of the business. It's important to know strengths and weaknesses. How can we get better if we do not collaborate and strive to be better?

Mentoring and encouragement pave the way for the next ingredients in a strong culture—gratitude and appreciation.

CHAPTER SIX

Nothing Replaces Appreciation and Gratitude

I could never have taken my business as far as I have without the help of my team. Honestly, I'm a pretty independent person. I don't mind eating alone in a restaurant, and my psyche doesn't need a team to feel complete. On the other hand, I've learned I do need a team to be better.

I grew up in a home full of support. My parents came to every school event and encouraged us every step of the way. Even Tom and Sherri demonstrated tremendous love and unwavering support. They stepped in for my parents and have been there for me every moment since I lost my mom and dad. This idea of beautiful support is the kind of culture I want my team to experience. I want them to feel supported and valued.

Appreciate Them

After I had the systems and processes in place, we quickly grew to a team of six. During that first year, as the holidays approached, I wanted to do something fun for them so they could feel that support I had known all my life. Since we have an entirely female team, I thought a team trip would be perfect.

We had reached some major goals that year, and every person had worked hard. I just wanted to show my appreciation.

At one of the last meetings of the year, the entire group gathered around the conference room table. At each seat, I had placed a small gift bag with a leather passport cover inside.

"I am so thankful for how hard you all work. You are all so committed to excellence. I just want to reward you. For the holidays, I want to say thank you."

The ladies opened their gifts, and I continued. "The entire team is going on a trip to Tulum, Mexico." The room went silent. I expected excitement and noise, maybe some dancing. For just a minute, I didn't know what to think. But when I scanned the room, I understood. All around, I saw tears—tears of gratitude. They were stunned. No one had ever acknowledged them this way before. In that instant, I realized just how important it is to say thank you and to recognize each individual's hard work in big, unexpected ways.

I truly believe this has been another pivotal piece in my ability to grow a strong, highly effective team. I haven't always had a large team; however, since those first six women came on board, we've consistently been mighty. We outproduce teams three to five times our size. And I think one of the driving factors in our success is this culture of thankfulness and appreciation.

I had an out-of-state colleague call me years ago. She had just experienced a mass exodus in her business. Her entire team left. She was devastated.

I asked her a bunch of questions to help her get to the bottom of the problem, and we discovered she didn't know the pulse of her team. She'd never taken time to get feedback from those she worked with. Like so many entrepreneurs and corporate managers, she had tunnel vision. Focused on sales and the health of the company, she didn't know what was happening with her team.

Without the right support, team members become unhappy. They may become jealous if someone gets more leads or one person receives promotions over another. Though the typical human resources question is, "What value does this individual bring to our team," as owners and managers, we have to ask, "What value do I bring to my team members?"

I am affiliated with Compass, and I truly love the fact that Robert Reffkin, the CEO, always says he works for the agents. He grows the company each day to deliver better results to his agents so they can be of more value to their clients. It is your duty to serve the people who work WITH YOU each day. The key is to serve their growth, their future, their career, and their spirits so they enjoy work and life. By serving them, your clients feel it, and your results as a company go to the next level.

Some team leaders say, "I teach my team how to succeed in our industry." Great, most groups or teams do that. What else do you do? Some walk through their company's vision, put check marks beside the values, and think that's enough. Others believe their great systems and processes should make people want to stick around.

When you get the right blend of people around you, you need to understand their personal goals. Ask each person, "What's your why?" To be effective leaders, we need to know our team members' professional and personal goals. It's imperative to know who they are. What drives them?

This kind of inventory allows us to reach them where they are, see where they want to be, and craft a plan to help them get there. Our teams have to be able to trust us. Honest feedback is priceless.

Someone once asked, "What if a member of your team is driven to run their own team someday?"

I say, "Support them. Give them your best." Do you remember the promise I make to every person who signs on to the team? "You will be a better professional on the day you leave than on the day you walk in." I want them to know every aspect of the industry.

One of the reasons I mentioned Cat earlier is because she's one who I knew very early on wouldn't be with me long. Not because she wasn't a good fit, but because she consistently went above and beyond any goals and had an entrepreneurial mindset. After a few years, I stopped providing her with leads. She had friends moving in from Chicago and had developed her own network. I finally took her aside and asked why she hadn't stepped out on her own. After all, she had been with us for years.

She had only one reason—she loved the team!

Cat stayed with us for nearly five years, but she did eventually move into her own space and does quite well as a solo agent. And I couldn't be happier for her. When you hire the best and bring your best, there's always that chance they'll branch out. But the value they bring while they're with you far outweighs the loss you feel when they move on. Providing value to your team means they appreciate you, which in turn brings value back to your company. This return on investment is not why you do it; it's merely a perk.

As business leaders who want to expand, it's imperative to not only hire the right people but invest in them. In our world of remote offices, and especially in the world of real estate, where many of our appointments are on the road, investing might take a bit more energy. But, whatever it takes, it will be worth it. In the Culture Guide at the end of the book, I've included a list of suggestions to inspire you as you appreciate your team and create a culture of nurture, admiration, and gratitude. But don't let that list limit you. Use it as a springboard to have fun with your team and Capture the Culture.

I want my team to understand how much they deserve recognition for their hard work and how important they are to the success of the company. Together, we are greater than individual parts. This mentality has propelled us into being one of the most successful and productive real estate teams in the country, and I think it stems from nurturing the culture daily.

Don't Be Afraid to Create Meaningful Appreciation

When it comes to nurturing a team that feeds into the culture, we need to create meaningful moments of appreciation. Every successful business is built on the back of its best team members, and if we fail to recognize that simple fact, we'll skimp. And when we skimp on our team, we skimp on our culture.

I dreaded some of those jobs on the farm. Does anyone really like cutting thistles out in the backfield? It meant hours and hours building up calluses on your hands. And it seemed like it was always ninety degrees on the days we sheared the cattle. The black hair stuck to every inch of exposed skin. Putting up hay always fell during those hottest days, too. And if you didn't wear jeans and long sleeves, the dried grassy stuff left something like little paper cuts all over your arms and legs. But the farm was the first place I learned, "Some days are dirt, some days are diamonds.[IP]" Fortunately, most days are diamonds, and when we focus on the positive, we focus on the diamonds.

This is a message Loren, one of my agents, brought to the team years ago. It doesn't matter how perfect your culture is, you'll have days that feel like dirt. It's vital to remember more diamond days are coming, and they come more often than the dirt days.

At a holiday party a few years back, I used this philosophy as an opportunity to show my appreciation.

Every year, I try to do something special. I want my team to know they deserve to be appreciated. Inspired by our dirt and diamonds reminder, I purchased a gift for each woman to remind them how special they are to me.

I began with a toast to the ladies reminding them that though we'd faced some days of dirt in the past year, we'd also had many days of diamonds. And as I finished, I said, "I always want you to know that you are strong and brilliant, and I never want you to lose your sparkle. Like diamonds, you are really tough, and I want you to know that each one of you is extremely precious to me."

Then, I sat a small gift box in front of each of them. Inside, they found simple diamond bracelets.

"Every time you look at this, I want you to be reminded that you are like diamonds to me. I never want you to dim or lose your sparkle. Never forget how valuable you are." It was a meaningful gift—one with a message of support and appreciation above all.

Depending on your budget or industry, you might not be able to be quite as extravagant; however, we should never be afraid to give an unexpected and meaningful gift. The trips I have gifted to team members over the years have been some of the best team-building experiences you could ever imagine. Remember, it's more how you make people feel. The most impactful thing you'll ever do might be sitting across the table from someone and telling them, "You're a rockstar. I don't know how you do what you do, but I couldn't do it without you."

I stopped one of our junior agents in the hall not long ago. She's hitting it out of the park, selling exponentially more in her first year than the norm.

"Do you know how well you're doing?" I asked.

"I couldn't have done it without you, Erin."

"I don't think you understand. This is all you. I might be giving you the opportunities, but you're grabbing them all. You've taken everything you've learned and pushed yourself to the next level."

These quick conversations will feel meaningful to people who've never had a CEO or manager congratulate them before. Meaningful appreciation can be something as simple as taking your time to give them a hand-written note or being exceedingly flexible with work schedules. A surprise day off, a cash bonus, or an unexpected gift "just because" will mean the world to your hardest-working members. Finding people who will give a hundred ten percent isn't easy, so don't let their dedication go unnoticed.

Have Fun

When you do everything with a smile and add fun to your culture, even the bad days become good days because you're in it together. From our annual team getaways—which the team only gets when we reach our goals—to fun gifts, office cheers, and being part of one another's lives, the comradery we create helps us stay positive even when we've had one of those dirt days.

Whether it's a team lunch, an evening at an escape room, a "Kudos Wall," or announcing a team win at a meeting, it's important to give your team members a chance to celebrate with each other. When you set the example of recognition, the entire team will become a place of encouragement. Giving them a place to put those shout-outs adds to this culture of appreciation.

Yes, we work hard. Because we're in sales, we have to make ourselves available. You never know what opportunity may await you when the phone rings. I set high expectations for myself as well as my team. But I truly want them to enjoy what they do. I have this tremendous team of real estate ninjas who have a reputation for doing good work that sets them apart from the rest. But even more importantly, they are fun. Our culture includes humor and funny moments. Even on the rough days—or maybe especially on the rough days—we just need to laugh.

I feel tremendous contentment with my life, and I want that for every member of my team. We work hard together, play hard together, and create an atmosphere of gratitude and appreciation that not only nurtures them; it nurtures me.

PART THREE
Monitor Actively

CHAPTER SEVEN

And Finally, You Protect It

Just because you've developed a culture of growth, integrity, knowledge, hustle, and nurture doesn't mean you can expect it to maintain itself. Adding staff, economic drops, and changes in the landscape can all affect the culture. Capturing the culture means protecting it at all costs. We have to constantly check the temperature of the team and keep ourselves in check if we want the culture we've built to continue to undergird our businesses.

The Erin Krueger Team has committed to a culture of excellence. On the day someone joins the team, they know everyone is prepared to help them become a better professional on the day they leave than on the day they come in. I tell them we're going to work hard together and have fun, and this commitment sets the tone for what our company will do for the new person as well as what we expect from them in the future.

I have an open-door policy and lead a forum where the entire team works to make sure everyone feels comfortable being honest. Even my interns learn very early that they have permission to speak up in our team meetings or approach me personally. Although I'm the ultimate decision-maker, I like to listen to all sides, possibly even run it by the two that ground me—Georgia and Sarah, and then choose which way to go.

Monitoring is a Must

The processes we created in the beginning have become invaluable as we grow. The checklists define our culture and keep us grounded. It's important to go back to those basics on a regular basis.

We use a Five-Step Audit Process[IP] to make certain our culture remains unchanged.

1. Define Desired Culture
2. Collect Data from the Team to Identify the Current Culture
3. Analyze the Data
4. Create an Action Plan that Identifies the Weaknesses
5. Regularly Monitor and Reassess the Culture

I've included all the details in the Culture Guide, but this overview will get you started. We continually tweak our checklists and refine our processes. Often, the client will feel as though they had a seamless experience, but in the background, things didn't go well. So, we look for ways to tighten up the process or system.

The bigger the team grows, the more difficult it becomes to see and hear each person in your organization. Regardless of our size, we want the culture to remain or grow into something better, and this only happens when each person feels valued. That's what makes the second step in our process so important. A team-first mentality only comes because we emphasize the crucial role of each individual.

In a remote office, this might mean a few extra questions when you do your culture check. When was the last time the team was together? Are we doing too much virtual and not enough in person? Is it time to do something so we can sit down face-to-face or as a reward opportunity?

In the beginning, I worked side-by-side with each team member. Today, I have close contact with several on my team daily, and while I meet with the others on a regular basis, I don't get to have as much one-on-one time with every single member. Still, I don't want the culture to change just because we're growing. I believe being involved in the lives of the team is a tremendously high priority.

It's important to me to not only keep my finger on the pulse of the company but also stay up-to-date with what's going on in the lives of my team. I want every person in our organization to feel like they can come to me. I never want them to think their opinion isn't valued.

As the team expands, being intimately involved with each member becomes challenging. Fortunately, my lead team members understand what it means to Capture the Culture and maintain it. Plus, because they spend more time with the other team members, they get a feel for their expectations and dreams. They know what's going on in their homes and hear the stories that accompany their pains and their joys. And when there's something important—whether it's an exciting milestone or a friction that needs resolution—they let me know so I don't miss the most important events. When you have a team with a collaborative spirit in an environment that allows every member to feel empowered, you end up with a significant number of complementary partners rather than employees and 1099 contractor agents.

We hire based on one-day, one-week, thirty-, sixty-, ninety-day check-ins. This is more than an evaluation, so it adds another level of intentional culture monitoring. We want to hear how our new team members feel about the atmosphere, the support they receive, and whether they have what they need to reach their goals.

You'll read books telling you to be ultra-involved in the lives of every person in your organization and others who advise you to keep your staff at arms' length and keep it professional. Neither advice is good or bad. You have to decide what kind of culture you want to have with your team and then build on it. I choose to let my team members know I'm there for them. I know they won't take advantage of me because our hiring process, though it takes a great deal of time, finds people who fit our culture. And when I do make a mistake, we have another team philosophy—"Slow to hire, quick to fire."

Be Prepared to Hear What You Don't Want to Hear

But what if those quarterly evaluations and the expectation of honesty backfire? What happens when they tell you what you don't want to hear?

That's going to happen sometimes. Georgia has been providing honest and valuable feedback since she joined the team—even when her truth is hard to hear. I talk too fast—especially when I've had a little too much caffeine. I don't do things the way other people do them. She knows me well, and she calls me out when I cross a line or consider a plan that doesn't match our culture. It can be an ego-buster for many entrepreneurs and managers, but if you want a culture that makes you better tomorrow than you are today, you have to be open to ideas, suggestions, and criticisms that don't make you feel warm and fuzzy.

Many don't know how to handle negative remarks, especially when they come from the newest member of the team. But the first rule of monitoring the culture is to listen and digest.

What they say may be unpleasant, but most often, if you've done your due diligence in hiring, you'll find truth in the constructive criticism. How can you make adjustments if you aren't willing to hear suggestions?

There is no such thing as a perfect manager. We are all humans, and as humans, we make mistakes. Maybe we miss the mark, don't give a team member the kudos they deserve, or neglect a shoutout in front of their peers. If you miss the mark and it affects a team member, you listen to their concerns and internalize. How can I be better, how can I do better, and how can I not make this mistake again? I care deeply for each person who works with me. I, too, have been on the end of missing the mark, and when it hurts a team member, I take that as a learning opportunity. I look for a way to be better, and I simply tell them I am sorry and will do better. Each person on my team deserves honesty, sincerity, and transparency, and open dialogue is the key to a solid foundation for any organization big or small.

Every time I meet with my team, whether as a group or one-on-one, we're crafting a plan on how the person or the organization can improve. What do we need to tweak to be better? Where does the team need to pivot? Like any vehicle on the road, sometimes we need to change direction to avoid a collision or reroute to get to an even better destination.

You can't expect members of your team to be willing to do the hard work of improving if you're not willing to craft a plan to be your best self as well. An open-door policy leads to transparency and honesty. Don't be afraid to create a positive change checklist for yourself as well as the members of your team. When the individuals you work with know they can provide feedback regardless of who their words call out and share their opinion when they sense something needs adjusted in the pulse of the company, you create a place where people feel valued, and they tend to stick around.

Every personality is different. We have team members from recent college grads to those looking to retire in a few years. Learning how to deal with each one can be overwhelming; however, when they know they can be as honest with you as you are with them, you open the floodgates for a strong culture and productive work environment.

What If It Doesn't Work Out

I'm not so naïve that I believe every team member will be with us forever. Some will grow and fly the nest. Others will be with us for a short span or a decade or more. And as sad as it sounds, we have had to part ways with some tremendous people who traveled through seasons of life that changed them.

As much as we care for our team members, we can't sacrifice culture when a team member's mindset or attitude changes because of life events or influence from outside sources. When we notice this shift, we spend time nurturing and mentoring, but sometimes, a person can become a toxic team member. It doesn't matter how much they contribute to the bottom line; if someone begins to break down the culture, we may have to part ways. Capturing the Culture is vital to the success of team members.

When a team member begins to negatively impact the culture, I take immediate action by addressing the issue through a structured process. First, I set up a meeting to see if a simple discussion can get to the bottom of what is going on. I take the time to reinforce that I choose them and I believe in them, so we need to work through whatever is going on. Being clear and intentional gives us an opportunity to get back on track. Sometimes, a simple meeting can turn things around. A leader or manager should never be afraid to have difficult conversations. It is imperative to the overall success and culture of the organization.

If their performance meets expectations but their attitude or mindset has shifted, I place them on a Performance Improvement Plan (PIP). This plan provides a clear framework and a thirty-day window for them to refocus and realign with the team's values.

For team members who have been with me for years and find themselves suddenly struggling—perhaps due to personal challenges or changing priorities—I approach the situation with empathy and options. If I believe the issue can be resolved, I offer them a choice. They can commit to the PIP and work to regain alignment, or they can take a three-month sabbatical to regain clarity, during which they refer their business to another team member.

When improvement seems impossible, or they choose not to pursue the offered paths, they must leave the team immediately. Protecting the culture of the team is non-negotiable, and sometimes that means making tough decisions to preserve the values and dynamics that allow us to thrive.

For example, trust is non-negotiable when it comes to my vendors. If a vendor arrives late once, I give them the benefit of the doubt—life happens. But if it happens again, it signals that my clients are not a priority to them. While I extend grace the first time, repeated issues without resolution show me that the relationship isn't aligned with the standards I uphold. At that point, I make the decision to stop working with them.

This approach may seem harsh to some, but it's rooted in a deep commitment to protecting my clients. Our culture is great service, and our preferred vendors are an extension of the team. We safeguard our culture because it's the foundation that allows us to consistently improve, evolve, and thrive. Our culture isn't just vital to the company's success— it's instrumental to the personal and professional growth of every individual on the team.

CHAPTER EIGHT

It's Time to Capture the Culture

I love helping others become their best selves, and I believe Capturing the Culture needs to be the number one ingredient in knowing who you are and where you want to end up. I meet people every day who haven't defined their business plan further than the dollars it will take to get it off the ground. Whether you are a solopreneur or you want to build a large company, your success begins with culture.

Think Differently

I believe my background has given me a unique perspective on life and business. For instance, I have a succession plan for my company. I'm sure I wouldn't have thought about that at such a young age if I hadn't lost my parents so suddenly. But I have a dozen families who count on our company for their livelihood. This business has to keep going even after I'm gone. Part of the culture is caring for my team, and that means looking out for them in the event something happens to me.

The biggest strategy boost leaders get when they Capture the Culture is the ability to think differently. Many I've talked to who thought being a solo agent or a one-person business have adjusted their view after I shared how much growth I experienced after I started developing a team. You can scale much faster and further when you have a group of people who share your values and embrace your team culture.

Many entrepreneurs make major mistakes when they begin team building. They hire the first people who apply. Then when it doesn't work out, they get discouraged and convince themselves being on their own would be better.

Currently, I have eight licensed agents and four on my admin team. But together, we are able to easily do the work of thirty-five because we hire based on our culture. That synergy creates a platform to produce at a very high level. Each person steps up to support the others. We genuinely care about each other. When I ask them to do something, they never turn me down. Not because they feel obligated but because they know if I ask, I need help, and I believe they can do it. Our culture of mutual respect means they know I worry about letting them down as much as they worry about letting me down.

Another mental shift many need to make is their focus on the bottom line. I have always said my greatest asset on the team is our culture. Our financial bottom line is important, even vital. But if you don't have a strong culture that you continually monitor, it can have a direct effect on your bottom line. Happy employees and team members allow businesses to flourish and reach those stretch goals because the culture is strong.

If you started a business, it's probably because it's something you were passionate about. I know I love what I do, and when I start to make a deal, I rarely spend a lot of time thinking about how much I will make. I know going into what the client needs to get out of it, and that's my focus. Whether I'm selling a $400,000 home or a $20,000,000 estate, my attitude remains steady. I'm passionate about serving my clients. I don't think about my commission. I focus on helping the client achieve their goals. When I concentrate on their needs and provide excellent service, profits follow.

Remain Grateful

When we keep our eyes on our passion, we have more fun and pass on that attitude to our team. This frees our team to simply do their best for the client rather than worry about the sale. On top of that, it allows us to make every client feel equally important. When my team puts an emphasis on the higher commission properties, our sellers sense it. They'll feel less important.

When I overhear someone talking about real estate at the grocery store, I'll interject. After the person realizes I'm knowledgeable about the subject, they ask for my card. But even more than my knowledge, they can tell I care about them and love what I do. It's not a typical business mindset, but it keeps my job interesting.

Holiday parties bring me some of my best leads. I love to meet new people, and most folks love to talk about real estate. I usually leave with a couple of contacts, but the reason they call me later is because my enthusiasm inspired them. People crave positivity.

This doesn't mean you have rose-colored glasses. It means we know better days are ahead. Through all my trageies, I've never asked, "What else could go wrong?" Even if it seems like a horrific tragedy, it can always be worse.

I remember flying to Denver just after my dad died. Some of his friends in the cattle industry were doing an auction to help raise funds to cover the expenses we had with the farm and my mom's care. It was the first time in my young life that I had flown when I wasn't heading somewhere for fun.

My perspective took a huge shift as I realized every time I got on a plane, there were people heading to unpleasant destinations. Not everyone on board was heading toward Disney or grandma's house for vacation. I realized life was like that plane. We're all on a journey together, and on any given day, some of the folks I meet are having tremendous days while others face horrible trials. A culture of gratitude, even when I'm going through the rough days, helps me have empathy and pick up the pulse of the people I'm interacting with.

On the good days and the bad days, I've learned staying thankful for where I am—we also call it keeping your positive pants on—is the important thing. I have fourteen hundred minutes every day, so why would I allow a troubling thirty- or sixty-minute meeting ruin the other thirteen hundred?

When I got married, I could have focused on the fact my mom and dad's seats were empty. Single roses marked their spots. Rather than be negative, I chose to be grateful for the twenty-one years I had with them and for Tom and Sherri. They were the ones who stepped up when others stepped out. My dad's six-foot-two best friend was also a huge teddy bear. He was unbending about truth and authenticity. I'm grateful for them and the other truth-tellers in my life.

One of the buyer's agents on my team recently did a stressful deal. She and the seller's agent were like oil and vinegar. My team member is very by the book, and the other agent was very lax. After close, we had a terrible time getting the keys and the codes to the gates. The sellers were supposed to disarm all the alarms, but that didn't happen. When they entered the property for the first time, every alarm went off. The experience was not smooth.

A week or more later, the selling agent called. The seller had left seven cable boxes in the house and wanted to swing by and pick them up. But the new owner had been through enough. They didn't want to deal with the previous owner again. So, my agent called the selling agent and communicated that they couldn't get the boxes.

It got so bad I finally had to get involved. The selling agent's team lead called me to try to work something out. I took the position of gratitude. "You know, I just want to take a moment and say how grateful and thankful our team is to have been able to be a part of a multimillion-dollar transaction. Your team got a great price per square foot. It was a record-breaking sale, right? And now we're arguing over seven fifty-dollar boxes. I know not every deal is flawless, and this one had its share of problems, but at the end of the day, our agents got it done. We're not going to inconvenience the buyer any more than they already have been. It's time to be thankful and move on. Don't you think?" The entire situation just needed someone to view it through eyes of gratitude.

Keep Growing

We can never stop growing. When we reach a milestone, we have to push the goal out a bit further. To accomplish this, our team dedicates two hours a week on training. Our senior agents lead the first hour of these focused sessions and I take the second. We script and share valuable insights and updates on the latest trends and strategies in real estate. This initiative fosters a culture of continuous learning and ensures we remain at the forefront of industry advancements.

Growing also means we never stop dreaming, and we can't give up even if it takes twenty years for us to reach the dream.

As we prepared to sell the farm during my senior year of college, I had a vision for the future. I had no idea I'd be in real estate or living in Nashville. But I knew I loved my dad's farm. So, I kept some embryos from his Triple Crown-winning Angus herd and paid to have them frozen for the past twenty years.

As I put the final touches on this book, that dream will come to fruition. My husband and I bought a fifty-acre farm right outside of Nashville, and soon, those embryos will be calved out, and my dad's herd will be in the field.

We're calling our new home Willow Creek Farm. It's because while those rigid oak trees will eventually crack and break when the pressure of storms of life get too much, the willows bend under the weight but always bounce back stronger than ever. It's a metaphor for my life and a picture of the culture I want to create.

I can't wait to see my dad's herd living the good life on our farm. It will be a full-circle moment for me.

Your visions don't all have to be business-related, but they do need to push you to growth. I seldom read when I was in high school and college. Now, I devour about a hundred books a year. Changing and adapting can be very uncomfortable, but when your culture makes personal growth a priority, you'll see those moments that cause you to bend and pivot through the eyes of appreciation.

Work with Erin Krueger and Her Team

If you look us up, you'll find The Erin Krueger Team holds one of the top positions for medium-sized teams in the state of Tennessee, but honestly, that doesn't matter much to me. We want you to work with our team because we have a culture of excellence and integrity, because your deal matters to us regardless of the size, and because we have fun while we get the job done.

Our culture demands that we treat every client better than they would expect. Real Estate is a service industry, and we try to take that word service to the next level. Because we serve each other, we're more prepared to serve our clients. We've been poured into, so we have more to give.

I am extremely passionate about this idea of healthy culture, and I love talking about it—almost as much as I enjoy talking about real estate. I've featured the topic on several podcasts, and it's the focal point when I share at conferences or business seminars. From coaching agents and entrepreneurs to helping professionals build the strongest teams possible, teaching others to build a culture that allows them to scale and be better tomorrow than they are today brings me the greatest joy.

If you're trying to buy or sell property in Nashville, my team would obviously love to serve you, but even more, no matter where in the world you live, we would be honored to help you Capture the Culture and seize our secret to success.

One of the most impactful cards I received when my dad passed had a quote from Ralph Waldo Emerson on the front.

What is success?…

To laugh often and much; to win the respect of intelligent people and the affection of children; to earn the appreciation of honest critics and endure the betrayal of false friends; to appreciate the beauty; to find the best in others; to leave the world a bit better, whether by a healthy child, a garden patch or a redeemed social condition; to know even one life has breathed easier because you have lived. This is to have succeeded!

That last line struck a chord in my life, and the final line, "to know even one life has breathed easier," described my dad. He touched so many people and made a difference in the lives of more than he ever realized. Emerson's quote and hearing people share amazing stories about my dad's influence changed my perspective on the definition of success.

I decided I wanted that kind of success in my life. Nothing is more important than making a difference for my team, my clients, and those I have the privilege to meet. This is the heart of learning to Cultivate your Culture[IP].

Culture isn't something you do; it's something you cultivate and develop. Not every day will be a good day, but we have the assurance better days are coming. That attitude sets the foundation for a powerful and productive culture. When you and your team commit to an uncompromised culture of integrity, excellence, continuous growth, and shared purpose, you become unstoppable—making a lasting impact on the lives of those you serve.

While the rest of society lets circumstances, economics, pandemics, personalities, and more hold them back, you'll be propelled forward because you've done the work to Capture the Culture.

The Culture Guide[IP]

Ten Characteristics of a Culture-Driven Team[IP]

Building a strong team culture is essential for creating a thriving business in any industry. Here are ten key characteristics to focus on:

1. **Shared Vision & Purpose:** Every member of the team needs to understand and believe in the overall mission of the company. A clear, shared vision fosters a sense of purpose, aligns actions, and motivates teams to work toward common goals. Culture is often the backbone of long-term success. Even a high performer can drag down the morale, engagement, and creativity of a team if they don't align with the company's culture. A person who fosters collaboration, trust, and adaptability will positively influence those around them.

2. **Know Their Why:** What are your team members' whys? If you know their goals and what their love language is, you know how best to communicate, motivate, and inspire them to reach ultimate goals.

3. **Trust & Transparency:** Trust is the foundation of a strong team. Transparent communication, where leaders are open and honest, helps build mutual trust and creates an environment where people feel safe sharing ideas and concerns. The leaders lead from example and keep an open-door policy. The heartbeat of the organization can never be put on the back burner.

4. **Accountability:** A culture of accountability ensures that every team member takes ownership of their role and responsibilities. This breeds trust and ensures everyone is contributing to the success of the organization. You can be a leader who has hard conversations. Sometimes we make hiring mistakes, but we learn from them. Every day is a gift. We need to make the most of it.

5. **No Clones but Complementary Partners:** Embracing different backgrounds, perspectives, and ideas enriches the culture. It encourages creativity and innovation, helping the team find solutions from various angles. We share a common vision of being committed to being better tomorrow than today. It's part of our team culture and mission. We learn from experience, each other, and our clients.

6. **Open Communication:** A team culture that prioritizes clear, honest, and respectful communication empowers team members to share ideas, give feedback, and address challenges without fear of retribution. The vernacular of "we" and "our"—not "I"—permeates the culture.

7. **Collaboration over Competition:** While healthy competition can drive performance, prioritizing

collaboration ensures that team members work together to support one another rather than trying to outshine their peers. It creates a stronger bond and maximizes collective talent. Hiring the right people is key. Consistently keeping high performers who don't contribute positively to culture can lead to turnover, disengagement, and burnout within the team. This approach is usually unsustainable in the long run.

8. **Recognition and Appreciation:** Recognizing and rewarding the efforts and achievements of individuals boosts morale and reinforces desired behaviors. Regular appreciation cultivates a positive, motivating environment. Trips, spa days, gifts, and just telling someone in the middle of the day, "You are so good at what you do, and I appreciate all your hard work." Maya Angelou is right. People always remember how you make them feel.

9. **Adaptability (Ability to Pivot):** A great team culture is flexible and adaptable. The ability to pivot and embrace new ideas or ways of working helps a business stay competitive and resilient in a changing market.

10. **Attitude and Mindset:** Assembling those who have a positive attitude and a mindset that recognizes every day will have its challenges, but we are problem solvers and we will get it done. "Wear your positive pants" and "No negative Nellies" are key phrases we often say. My favorite is "Some days are diamonds, and some are dirt—but most are diamonds." There are fourteen hundred minutes in a day. Don't let a thirty-minute meeting make the entire day a bad day. Pull yourself up and move forward.

Creating a Culture of Appreciation and Recognition

My favorite Maya Angelou quote has always been: "I've learned that people will forget what you said, people will forget what you did, but people will never forget how you made them feel."

1. **Personalized Recognition**

   - **What:** Tailor recognition to the individual by acknowledging their specific contributions and personality.
   - **How:** Write a heartfelt handwritten note or make a public shout-out during a team meeting, highlighting their unique strengths and recent achievements.

2. **Growth and Development Opportunities**

   - **What:** Offer learning experiences that align with employees' career aspirations.

- **How:** Pay for a professional development course, send them to a conference, or provide access to a mentor in the field they want to grow in.

3. **Flexible Work Arrangements**

   - **What:** Give flexibility as a reward to help improve work-life balance.
   - **How:** Offer a "remote day" where employees can work from anywhere or give them the option of adjusting their hours for a week.

4. **Surprise Time Off**

   - **What:** Give employees an unexpected day off to relax and recharge.
   - **How:** Send them home early on a Friday after a project's completion, or give them a "surprise holiday" to show appreciation for their hard work.

5. **Team Celebration Outings**

   - **What:** Celebrate successes with experiences that bring the team together.
   - **How:** Organize a fun, team-building outing like an escape room challenge, a team lunch at a favorite restaurant, or a cooking class where the whole team can unwind.

6. **Recognition Wall or Kudos Board**

   - **What:** Create a visible place where team members can publicly appreciate each other.

- **How:** Set up a "Kudos Wall" in the office (or a digital version) where employees can leave notes or shout-outs for their peers. This encourages a culture of continuous recognition.

7. **Custom Gifts**

- **What:** Reward employees with a thoughtful, personalized gift.
- **How:** Instead of generic rewards, give each employee something meaningful, such as a favorite book, hobby-related item, or personalized office supplies like custom notebooks or mugs. If you are a close group, you will know what they like or covet. A gift they would never get themselves is something they will treasure.

8. **Exclusive Leadership Opportunities**

- **What:** Provide opportunities to take on new responsibilities or lead a project.
- **How:** Recognize employees by offering them leadership roles in new initiatives or giving them the chance to head a key project, showing trust in their abilities.

9. **Peer-to-Peer Recognition Program**

- **What:** Implement a system where employees can recognize and reward each other.
- **How:** Create a peer-nominated monthly award where employees nominate someone they believe

has gone above and beyond. Offer a small prize or public recognition to the winner.

10. **Trips or Monetary gifts**

- **What:** Show appreciation by investing in an elaborate trip or a cash bonus.
- **How:** Provide a trip either as a team building activity, where you build comradery, or offer trip incentives as a well-earned trip for team building or a cash bonus for them to do with what they want.

These ideas go a long way toward showing team members they are valued and respected, fostering a positive and motivated work environment. Regularly incorporating them can build a culture of appreciation and long-term commitment.

The Culture Audit[IP]

The culture audit is an intentional, systematic review of your team's dynamics, values, and engagement. It's a way to take a step back and evaluate—is the company culture thriving, or are there areas that need attention? This process involves gathering and analyzing data and making adjustments to realign your company with your desired culture. Here's how to conduct a thorough culture audit:

Step 1: Define the Desired Culture[IP]

Before diving into an audit, clarify what culture you're aiming to cultivate. This means defining:

- **Core Values:** What are the guiding principles of your company? (e.g., integrity, innovation, collaboration)
- **Behavioral Norms:** What behaviors do you want to see regularly in your workplace? (e.g., open communication, mutual respect, accountability)
- **Leadership Expectations:** How do you expect leaders to interact with the team and guide the company?

- **Employee Experience:** What does a positive employee experience look like in your ideal culture?

Establishing these benchmarks provides you with a reference point when evaluating the current culture.

Step 2: Collect the Culture Data[IP]

To get a full picture of your company's culture, gather a mix of both qualitative (personal insights, stories) and quantitative (numbers, metrics) data. Here's how:

1. **Employee Surveys:**

   - Create anonymous surveys with questions about team morale, satisfaction, leadership effectiveness, and work-life balance. Use Likert scales (e.g., 1-5 ratings) for easier analysis.
   - Include open-ended questions to encourage employees to share thoughts on what's working and what's not.

2. **One-on-One Interviews:**

   - Have confidential conversations with employees across various levels. Ask about their experiences, what they enjoy about the workplace, and areas they think need improvement.
   - Probe deeper into specific cultural aspects like collaboration, respect, and communication. Sometimes, employees are more candid in a face-to-face conversation than in a survey.

3. **Focus Groups:**

   - Conduct small focus groups with teams or departments to discuss cultural themes. This is useful for getting different perspectives on the same issues and fostering honest dialogue.

4. **Leadership Interviews:**

   - Interview team leaders or managers to assess their views on the company's culture and their role in shaping it. Ask them how they feel about their leadership style, team engagement, and alignment with company values.

5. **Data Analysis:**

   - Look at HR data such as employee turnover, absenteeism, and performance metrics. High turnover or disengaged employees can indicate culture issues.
   - Examine hiring trends: are you attracting talent that aligns with your values? Are candidates staying long-term?

6. **Exit Interviews:**

   - Review past exit interview notes to identify patterns in why employees are leaving. Are they departing because of cultural misalignment, lack of growth opportunities, or leadership issues?

Step 3: Analyze the Culture Data^{IP}

After collecting your data, it's time to identify trends and patterns:

1. **Look for Consistencies:**

    *   Are there recurring themes in feedback across different teams or departments? For instance, do multiple employees mention communication breakdowns or lack of recognition?
    *   Compare employee feedback with leadership perspectives—are there gaps between how leadership perceives the culture and how employees experience it?

2. **Assess Key Metrics:**

    *   What do the hard numbers tell you? Metrics like engagement scores, employee retention, and absenteeism can help quantify the state of your culture.
    *   Compare the results to industry benchmarks if available.

3. **Highlight Strengths and Weaknesses:**

    *   Pinpoint areas where your culture is thriving. For example, if employees rate high on collaboration and innovation, celebrate that.
    *   Also, highlight pain points where your culture is faltering. If there's a significant disconnect

between management and employees, or if employees feel undervalued, note that for action.

Step 4: Create a Culture Action Plan[IP]

Once the audit is complete, it's time to act on your findings:

1. **Reinforce Strengths:**

   - Build on what's already working. If teamwork and communication are strong, find ways to foster them further, perhaps by implementing more collaborative projects or team-building exercises.

2. **Address Weaknesses:**

   - Prioritize the cultural gaps identified during the audit. For example, if the data shows a lack of recognition, create a formal recognition program to regularly celebrate wins.
   - Develop initiatives to align behavior with company values. This could involve training managers on leadership styles that reflect company values or implementing new communication tools to enhance transparency.

3. **Set Clear Goals:**

   - Establish specific, measurable goals to improve your culture. For instance, aim to increase employee engagement scores by ten percent in six months or reduce turnover by fifteen percent in the next year.

- Assign responsibility for these initiatives to individuals or teams to ensure follow-through.

Step 5: Monitor and Reassess the Culture^{IP}

Culture is dynamic, and it's essential to continuously monitor and reassess it:

1. **Implement Pulse Surveys:**

   - Conduct regular, shorter surveys (e.g., quarterly or biannually) to keep track of the cultural changes and check if implemented initiatives are effective.

2. **Hold Feedback Sessions:**

   - Encourage ongoing feedback from employees through open-door policies, suggestion boxes, or scheduled check-ins.

3. **Revisit the Audit:**

   - Conduct a full culture audit every year or two to ensure your culture stays aligned with your company's evolving goals.

A culture audit is a powerful tool to identify where your organization stands culturally and how you can close the gap between where you are and where you want to be. By approaching this with transparency, humility, and a commitment to improvement, you will cultivate a culture that supports your business goals and empowers your team to thrive.

About the Author

Erin Krueger is a nationally recognized leader in real estate, known for her innovative approach, dynamic leadership, and unwavering commitment to excellence. With nearly two decades of industry experience and a background in advertising and marketing, Erin began her career as a solo agent and quickly rose to become Tennessee's top realtor, earning a spot among the nation's top professionals when she was ranked #14 in the nation.

Her drive and vision led her to build one of the country's most successful real estate teams—an award-winning powerhouse team ranked number one in Tennessee and #3 nationally by *The Wall Street Journal* and *RealTrends* for record-breaking achievements.

With over $2 billion in transactions, thousands of homes sold, and nearly $225 million in sales in 2024, Erin's success is rooted in her hands-on approach, strategic thinking, and passion for empowering others. Beyond real estate, she is dedicated to mentoring and coaching entrepreneurs, helping them turn vision into action and build thriving businesses.

Now, as a first-time author, Erin shares the hard-earned lessons, strategies, and personal experiences that have shaped her career. Her book serves as both a blueprint and an inspiration for those looking to rise above challenges, cultivate high-performing teams, and create a culture of success that transcends industries.

CONNECT WITH ERIN & HER TEAM

Take your next steps towards Capturing the Culture

Scan to Learn More

CAPTURE THE CULTURE

Interested in
additional tools
and resources?

Scan to
Access